MW00364644

Roots

From Outward Bound to Expeditionary Learning

Edited by
Emily Cousins

KENDALL/HUNT PUBLISHING COMPANY
4050 Westmark Drive   Dubuque, Iowa 52002

Cover Portrait of Kurt Hahn: Sara Hilby, a third-grade teacher at Lincoln Elementary School in Dubuque, Iowa.

Illustrations: All other illustrations were excerpted from a field guide created by seventh-grade students at King Middle School in Portland, Maine, for a learning expedition called "A Park Grows in Portland." The artists included in *Roots* are: Virgil Buzzell, Anthony Catbagan, Rachel Chom, Terra Parker, Annie Rodriguez, and Josh Sweetser.

Cover and interior design: Carroll Conquest, Conquest Design

ISBN 0-7872-7644-8

Library of Congress Catalog Card Number: 00-108599

Printed in the United States of America

10 9 8 7 6 5 4 3 2 1

ROOTS

FROM OUTWARD BOUND TO EXPEDITIONARY LEARNING

CONTENTS

Introduction

Greg Farrell

When Expeditionary Learning began as a project of Outward Bound in 1992, one trustee remarked that it was good to see Outward Bound returning to its roots in conventional schooling. Indeed, as Thomas James writes in "The Only Mountain Worth Climbing," Outward Bound "first took shape, pedagogically, as an educational innovation arising from a secondary school."

Outward Bound was originally a "short course" version of what its founder, Kurt Hahn, was trying to do every day, and over a period of years, with his students at Gordonstoun and Salem, the boarding schools he headed in Scotland and Germany. Now Expeditionary Learning is applying the philosophy of Outward Bound back to what we might call the "long course"—everyday kindergarten through twelfth-grade schooling.

As Expeditionary Learning teachers guide their students on that long course, they draw from almost sixty years of craft wisdom. For many years, educators have been taking Outward Bound courses in the wilderness and finding there a quality of teaching they could use in their own schools to improve teaching and learning. Expeditionary Learning emphasizes these practices in the extensive professional development it provides to whole faculties in schools that decide to adopt the Expeditionary Learning design. Here are some examples of practices used by Outward Bound instructors that teachers have adapted well to the classroom:

∼ PICKING PROJECTS THAT SEEM IMPOSSIBLE TO STUDENTS AND THEN ACCOMPLISHING THEM. On Outward Bound courses, students regularly climb mountains they do not think they can climb, or they hike hours longer than they think they can hike. In Expeditionary Learning schools, the best learning expeditions have this quality of "doing the impossible." Expeditionary Learning first graders in Denver have put on a production of the musical *Cats,* and second graders have built a faithful replica of Thoreau's cabin on their school grounds. Middle school students in Portland, Maine, have designed a new wing for their school.

∼ JOINING VERY HIGH STANDARDS WITH THE EXPECTATION THAT EVERYONE IS GOING TO SUCCEED AND HELP OTHERS SUCCEED. Outward Bound crews are deliberately diverse; but that does not mean that only the strongest or fittest will climb the mountain. The goal is to get everyone in the crew up the mountain together. Those who are weak in one area will be strong in another. In Expeditionary Learning schools, which were described by a professor at Denver University as "education for the gifted, extended to everyone," there is no tracking, and students collaborate with, critique, and help one another to do their very best work.

~ DOING A MINIMUM OF INSTRUCTION WITH A MAXIMUM OF APPLICATION. On Outward Bound courses, leaders instruct students in new skills: knot-tying; rock-climbing; paddling; orienteering; and building shelters. But instructors devote only a modest amount of time to this before they provide students with the necessity to apply their new skills. On a sea course, for example, the instructors at the Hurricane Island Outward Bound School teach students the basics of rowing, then tow their students' eight-oared boats out to sea, detach the boats, and ask the students to row back to shore on their own. Suddenly, all the abstractions of sailing skills have a concrete purpose—getting back to dry land. Expeditionary Learning teachers also use "ground school" to impart the basics, but they do not spend much time lecturing and showing before they have their students immersed in real-life applications.

~ BREAKING DOWN COMPLEX TASKS INTO SMALL STEPS. Outward Bound instructors are superb at this. They have to be, because their students are almost immediately going to "do something" with what they have learned, and the larger task is likely to be too overwhelming to grasp and apply all at once. Rappelling down a ravine for the first time can seem impossible, but when students learn step-by-step how to put on a harness, fasten caribiners, and communicate with their belayers, it can begin to seem possible. Teachers say the same process works well when students have to publish a book for a language arts project or submit an architectural plan to the city council.

⌒ WORKING IN SMALL GROUPS. The usual Outward Bound crew includes seven to ten people. Groups of this size help nourish and promote friendship, community, and accountability. Individual and group responsibilities become clear. Instructors pay attention to how the group is doing, but they also attend to how each individual is faring within the group and with regard to the particular task at hand. Teachers in Expeditionary Learning schools use small groups both to organize academic work and to make sure that no one gets isolated or lost in the shuffle.

⌒ MODELING WHAT YOU ARE TRYING TO TEACH. Outward Bound instructors have to live what they are teaching, or they lose credibility with their students. Instructors and students live so closely together on courses that it would become immediately apparent if an instructor had different standards of conduct for themselves and for their students. They have to walk their talk. This is also true of teachers in conventional schools. If they are not lit up by learning, there is little chance they will light up their students with the excitement of learning. The professional development we offer teachers gives them the experience of being students on learning expeditions in which our staff model the kind of teaching we want them to do.

In turn, the teachers model for their students the curiosity, compassion, and respect they foster in their classrooms.

~ CHANGING THE CONTEXT. On Outward Bound courses, students are thrust into environments where the rules and circumstances are radically different from what they are used to. They get up before the sun does. They walk through streams without stopping to take their boots off, then hike them dry. They learn to do with less, and begin to love it. Thus they experience and think about things in fresh and stimulating ways. Expeditionary Learning classroom teachers use a similar approach. For example, one group of seventh graders in Boston researched what to do with nearby vacant lots not by reading textbooks, but by getting into the unfamiliar worlds of the door-to-door interview, zoning committees, courthouses, and a graduate school of architecture.

~ GRADUALLY STEPPING BACK AND LETTING THE STUDENTS TAKE CHARGE. This is perhaps *the* fundamental pedagogical practice of Outward Bound instructors over the span of a typical course. When students first arrive on a wilderness course, they are dependent on the instructor, who is an expert in a realm where the students are novices and beginners. But as the course unwinds, and the students become more experienced and competent in the new environment, the instructor answers fewer questions and turns more of them back on the students, inviting and then requiring them to figure things out for themselves. Many teachers say they find letting go of control of the student work in this way at once the hardest and most exhilarating aspect of teaching in an Expeditionary Learning school.

Classroom teachers have been inspired by these practices on courses since Outward Bound began, but in the 1980s, Outward Bound decided that it was not enough to bring students and teachers to the wilderness for "short courses." Outward Bound decided to establish urban centers to make programs more available to urban youth and the people who work with them. The New York City Outward Bound Center, the Baltimore-Chesapeake Outward Bound Center, the Atlanta Outward Bound Center, and the Thompson Island Outward Bound Education Center in Boston not only brought more "short courses" to both students and teachers, but also developed sustained relationships with particular schools. These relationships brought Outward Bound's approach to teaching and learning into the curriculum, structure, and culture of these schools. In 1987, at the invitation of former dean of Harvard Graduate School of Education Paul Ylvisaker, Outward Bound and Harvard started a joint project on experience-based education.

In the 1990s, Outward Bound built on this work by launching an urban/education initiative. This was a deliberate search for the best and most replicable models for using Outward Bound's philosophy and programming to create and sustain institutional change. All the U.S. Outward Bound schools and urban centers were encouraged by the national organization to develop more sustained relationships and deeper programs with individual schools. Instructors adapted Outward Bound courses in the wilderness to teach reading and writing along with sailing and self-confidence. High school teachers modified English and History courses to incorporate fieldwork, adventure, and service. This experience, and the opportunity provided by the New American Schools Development Corporation in 1992 to think and work on using Outward Bound's ideas to improve the structure, culture, curriculum, and instruction in entire schools, led to the birth of Expeditionary Learning. We are now working with over ninety-five schools across the country and expect to be working with more than 200 schools by 2005.

Expeditionary Learning has drawn its ideas and practices from a variety of sources. But many of our central practices and beliefs—the teaching practices described above, the commitment to service, the focus on bringing out the best in people, the importance of craftsmanship, adventure, and active learning—have their roots in the life and work of Kurt Hahn. The articles and speeches included in this book provide a glimpse of Hahn and the schools he founded. They help to describe Outward Bound's journey from long course to short course and back again.

Greg Farrell is president and chief executive officer of Expeditionary Learning Outward Bound.

If One Cares Enough: Teaching at Hahn's School

Joshua Miner

In 1933, Outward Bound founder Kurt Hahn opened Gordonstoun, a boys' school in Scotland that became renowned as one of Britain's most distinguished progressive schools. Joshua Miner, an American teacher, taught at Gordonstoun in 1951–1952. Inspired by his work with Hahn, Miner returned home and, along with Charles Froelicher, helped to start Outward Bound in the United States. Since then, Miner has worked tirelessly to foster Hahn's ideas in wilderness schools, urban education centers, and public and private schools. In the following account, Miner describes what it was like to teach at Gordonstoun.

*T*he long twilight had only just set in when we arrived at Gordonstoun at 9:30. I had a sense of old buildings and long-tended landscaping, then the incongruity of several quonset huts. I was deposited at the door of the main building where a student was awaiting my arrival.

I was led inside and up a wide, highly polished central staircase. The student told me that this was Gordonstoun House, which had once been a castle, and that it was more than three centuries old. On the second floor the student knocked on a door. As it opened and I entered, Kurt Hahn shook my hand. A big man of perhaps 60 years, Hahn had great shoulders, somewhat stooped, and big hands giving a firm grip. He had large features and ears, and deep-set eyes with a full, live gaze. It was an extraordinary face, with experience, wisdom, and good will in its expression.

His first words were, "But my good man, you must be tired. You must sit down immediately."

I was quickly made aware of his omnivorous curiosity about people. Abetted by the three elderly ladies who were dining with him, he simultaneously plied me with questions and bade me eat. By the end of the meal he knew a great deal about me and my family. I remember well that I was cold—particularly that my feet were cold and damp—because of an incident during the meal. The student who had greeted me entered and spoke to Hahn. This was Humphrey Taylor, he told me, and if I would step out in the hall, Humphrey had something for me. What young

Humphrey had was a pair of my dry wool socks. I had no idea how the boy had received the word to fetch those socks. Nor did I realize that the fetching had required a four-mile round trip by bicycle to go to the guest house and extract the socks from my luggage. Humphrey informed me that he was the Helper of Guests. That was his post in the student hierarchy.

The next day, Humphrey Taylor gave me a good look at the school through a student's eyes. Humphrey told me about the Training Plan, which was the foundation of an elaborate system of student responsibility. It was a checkoff list of each student's daily routine, starting with the morning run, cold shower, and room chores, and so on through doing of assignments, attending classes, writing home, and bedtime teeth brushing. Once a student was judged ready to be responsible for himself, he made his own daily checkoff and carried out his own penalties for such infractions as being late for class. The prescribed penalty for lateness and other infractions was to get up early for an extra long run. I asked Humphrey why, since nobody checked on him, he did not just skip doing his lates, as he called them. "Come on, Humphrey," I said, "I would."

Humphrey smiled. "I used to," he said, "but I got tired of lying to myself." That sold me. I did not know if the Training Plan would work in an American school, but it was working here.

A few days later, Hahn sent me off to the Moray Sea School. The Moray Sea School was my first exposure to Outward Bound. No one called it that, however; I had not yet heard the name. Hahn and others simply referred to it as the short-term school. They explained to me that boys 14 to 18 came here for a twenty-eight-day course that was physically rugged and challenging, and in a general way I gathered that the purpose of the school was character building. Most of the boys were apprentices sent by industry, some were police cadets. A few were from correctional institutions or had been referred by social agencies.

That day, the next-to-last of the course, the boys were doing a final cross-country endurance test. Divided by age into groups of six, they had to travel cross-country, with the aid of map and compass, through a series of checkpoints in the moor wilderness. This was a difficult test in land navigation, for it is easy to get lost in the moors. The distance was twenty-eight miles for the oldest group and ranged down to twenty-two for the youngest, and they were to travel as rapidly as they could without breaking up the group.

These were youngsters from more or less disadvantaged backgrounds who had been born in the Depression years, and had grown while undergoing the privations of World War II. Their post-war, still-rationed diets had not enabled them to recover from a poor start. They were scrawny, undersize, and wiry. It was a real eye-opener that they could cover twenty-eight miles in a day, under pressure. I had never seen anything like it with boys in the States.

When we returned to Gordonstoun, we had dinner with Mr. and Mrs. Chew. As director of activities, Bobby Chew was one of the school's most important people. Hahn had a unique idea of what a school's staff structure should be. Under the headmaster were two men of equal rank—a director of studies and a director of activities. The one was responsible for the curricular program, the other for everything that did not take place in the classroom, which at Gordonstoun was a broad gamut. Hahn made the two posts equal because he felt the school should pay equal attention to the academic and nonacademic sides of a youngster's development. When one program encroached on the other, the other was expected to fight back; Hahn relished that seesaw tension between his two lieutenants.

On the flight home I studied and reflected on the Gordonstoun School Final Report to Parents. This was virtually a duplicate of the form Hahn had long ago developed at Salem, the school he started in Germany. Better than any other document, it encapsulated his educational concerns. The student was rated on his public spirit, sense of justice, and ability to follow out what he believed to be the right course in the face of various physical and psychological obstacles. Then came the report on his academic performance and, if he were a member of the Cliff Watchers, the Fire Service, or the Army or Sea Cadets, a service report by his command officer.

It was like no report card I had ever seen. For three decades, I reflected, this man had been doing things in education that I had merely dreamed of in a theoretical way, and had carried them far beyond the blurred limits of my wishful speculations. More than any other educator of whom I was aware, Hahn practiced the philosophy that education had a twin objective: to enable the student to make intelligent judgments and to develop the inherent strengths of his selfhood (to build character, in the old-fashioned phrase). The report to parents was the frame of reference that defined the goal Hahn had stated so stirringly years before: "To produce young people able to effect what they see to be right, despite hardships, despite dangers, despite inner skepticism, despite boredom, despite mockery from the world, despite emotion of the moment."

In October 1950, I wrote Hahn that I would like to return to Gordonstoun as a staff member the following year. He replied by cable: "Your suggestion thrills me." On February 15, 1951, the entire family—Phebe, our two infant daughters, and I—sailed on the *Parthia* for Liverpool.

My first teaching assignments at Gordonstoun included general science, current events, and what we would call a "remedial class" in arithmetic. The latter group was my first hands-on exposure to Hahn's working principle that a boy was not to be penalized for a deficiency over which he had no control. Two factors that should not prevail in denying admission to the school were a family's inability to pay and a boy's low I.Q. The important question was: What is the boy doing with his endowment? Many Gordonstoun students did splendidly in the university examinations. We also had some interesting youngsters who were far from what

SALEM SCHOOL FINAL STUDENT REPORT

At Hahn's Salem School in Germany, students were assessed according to the following criteria:

Esprit de corps

Sense of justice

Ability to state facts precisely

Ability to follow out what he believes to be
the right course in the face of discomforts,
hardships, dangers, mockery, boredom,
skepticism, and impulses of the moment

Ability to plan

Imagination

Ability to organize shown in the disposition of work
and in the direction of young boys

Ability to deal with the unexpected

Degree of mental concentration where the task in
question interests him, where it does not

Conscientiousness
in everyday affairs
in tasks with which he is specially entrusted

Manners

Manual dexterity

Standard reached in school subjects:
German   Natural Science
Ancient Languages   Mathematics
Modern Languages   History

Practical work (Handicraft, etc.)

Art work

Physical exercises
Fighting spirit
Endurance
Reaction time

would be considered academically qualified at most British or American schools.

Those boys in my special class were just about mathematically illiterate. Many of these lads had endured the bombing in the Battle of Britain, and undoubtedly some had suffered traumas. Emotional disturbances, manifested in such aberrations as bed-wetting, were then common among young Britishers. But in that arithmetic class was a socially powerful youngster who would win a place of leadership among the students. Another would become a master farmer, the greatest grower of tomatoes under glass in Great Britain; academia did not come easily for him, but he had fine common sense. A third was an artist, a genius in stained-glass design.

There were sons of bricklayers in the school who had aspirations different from their fathers', and there were others who intended also to be bricklayers. Both were equally honored. Hahn hoped the latter would go back into their world better bricklayers because they were better citizens. There were boys who were going to sea; their careers in the merchant service had already been chosen for them. They were honored at the same level as somebody destined for a university to become a doctor. It was a part of Hahn's greatness as a headmaster that he gave youngsters a sense of being members of a community in which all had the same opportunity to earn the same kind of respect from their peers. At the same time, he was on the alert for any kind of lateral shift an individual might develop. Here comes, say, a youngster who has a genius for working in stained glass but whose academic tickets are subpar. He is exposed to poetry and drama and music, and perhaps he will be enthused by one of these. Also, he is exposed to competition with others in a political sense, in the school governing structure. That could hardly happen to him if as a consequence of the Eleven Plus he had been diverted into a vocational stream.

Another of my early responsibilities was The Break. It was essential, in Hahn's thinking, that a healthy youngster "have his powers of resilience, coordination, acceleration, and endurance purposefully developed." The Break was his unique contribution to physical education. He had invented it in the early Salem days, and from the beginning had made it an imperative part of the Gordonstoun scheme. Four mornings a week, during a fifty-minute break in what Hahn called "the sedentary hours," each boy took part in two of a half-dozen events—sprinting or distance running, long or high jumping, discus or javelin throwing. A student competed only against himself, trying to better his previous best performance. The frail youngster who broke ten feet in the long jump for the first time in his life got as big a cheer as the track team star beating his previous mark at close to twenty. Every boy had to do every event. That same star jumper might be a dud at throwing the discus. It was as important to overcome a weakness as to develop a strength.

When I was put in charge of The Break, I became a fascinated witness to its remarkable results. It was not just that the average performance would have put the average American schoolboy to shame. The great satisfaction lay in seeing the physical duffer discover that through trying from day to day he could do much better than he would have dared to dream. He had learned, in Hahn's phrase, to "defeat his defeatism." You could see him shed—Hahn again—"the misery of his unimportance." His new-found confidence would carry over into his peer relationships, his classroom performance, the quality of work on his project. It was not unusual for a timid or sensitive boy with an undeveloped physique to emerge from the chrysalis of his underconfidence a competent athlete, surprised to find himself confirming what the headmaster had so often told the school: "Your disability is your opportunity."

As a housemaster, I learned firsthand about the Training Plan and the whole Gordonstoun scheme of student self-government. When Jones was a new boy at the school, an older student came to him each night and checked off his Training Plan. This was a list of questions that covered the gamut of Jones's daily duties, from taking his morning shower and doing his before-breakfast household chores, through completing his lessons and getting to classes on time, to brushing his teeth at night. To each query, Jones would answer yes or no, and for any shortcomings the older boy would mete out the prescribed penalties. In time, perhaps after three or four months, the older boy would decide that Jones had reached a state of responsibility where he could be entrusted with his own Training Plan and his own punishments. He would so report to McDonald, who as Helper of the House was Windmill Lodge's number one boy. McDonald would come to me and say, "I think it is time for Jones to take on his own Training Plan."

I would say, "What's the evidence? What makes you think Jones is ready?" And McDonald would say something like, "Well, sir, I'm satisfied that he is answering Williams honestly every night. And the other day something happened, and when I asked how it happened, he immediately popped up with all the facts, even though it involved him in some of the blame." So I would call Jones down and talk with him. If I was convinced, I would take the recommendation to the headmaster, who would give me a thorough grilling. I would have to have my facts and make a really good case for Jones.

Then, a month or so after he had been given his own Training Plan, I would say to Jones, "Get your Training Plan; I want to see it." Perhaps a look of horror would come over his face. He would jog over to the house and come back with his plan, on which he had made no entries for the past ten days. So he would have to go back down the line, and Williams would take over again. Then after a while McDonald would come once more and say it was time for Jones, and I would say, "Now look, don't get me in trouble again. Are you sure?" I would go to the head-master and he would say, "Are you sure?" I would be on trial, not Jones. So Jones would get his Training

Plan back, and this time when I checked up on him, it would be in good order, and Jones was well on his way to being a self-responsible member of the school community.

However tight the day's schedule, Hahn found time to reconnoiter about the school. "A headmaster's job," he said, "is to walk around." His antennae were always out, fine-tuned and waving, probing for each lad's potential strengths that they might be developed, for his innate weaknesses that they might be overcome. Repeatedly he homed in on some shielded aspect of a boy's ego that others had missed and that cast a sudden light on deviant behavior. He was part psychologist, drawing on a vast bank of personal observations.

Periodically, roused from slumber by Hahn's call, four or five of us—housemaster, teachers, activity leader—would make our way through the night to his study. The call would have but one meaning—some boy was in trouble. Perhaps a student had been caught stealing. Hahn would have spent a long evening getting the report, talking with the boy and with the student leaders who knew him best. Conscious of the contrast between our disheveled aspects and his neat daytime attire, we would wait for him to stop pacing the floor and tell us why we were there. Finally, when he had given us the facts, came the inevitable dreaded question, the blue eyes boring in: "Josh! When did you first notice this boy was in difficulty, and what did you do about it?"—dreaded because one had sensed and done nothing. When a boy was in danger of expulsion at Gordonstoun, it was not he but the adult community who was on trial. A boy steals because he has some deeper trouble. If one is sensitive enough, if one cares enough, one can detect symptoms of the trouble early, when there may still be time for remedy.

Hahn ran the school in tensile fashion. It began with his hiring strong people who would stand up to him. Offering Henry Brereton the post of director of studies in 1935, he said, "You must defend your department. If I want to send a boy into the hills for his health just before examinations, you must resist me." When I became director of activities, I found that Brereton and I were duty-bound to maintain a rival stance, lest either poach on the other's share of school time.

The same tensilizing principle infused his way with the young. His core tenet, stated a thousand times as though it were cut in bronze, was: "It is the sin of the soul to force young people into opinions—indoctrination is of the devil—but it is culpable neglect not to impel them into health-giving experiences." The indoor type was to be chased outdoors, the introvert turned inside out, and extrovert outside in. The tough were to be gentled, the timid emboldened. Above all, the complacent were to be disturbed. "It is my mission in life to molest the contentedly unfit."

Hahn had powerful ideas about which experiences were "health-giving." We did not play soccer (football, they called it) at Gordonstoun even though it was the Scottish national game, because Hahn felt the professional players, with their tactics of going for the man instead of the ball, had brutalized the sport. It was, in fact, another of his declared missions in life to "dethrone games," i.e., team sports. Games were good when they taught a lesson of "the good ally" and teamwork, modesty in winning, resolution in defeat. They did harm when they glorified individual performance, or brute power, and when they stifled other interests.

Once when I was coaching the track team, we had gotten off to a good start and built a lead in a meet at Gordonstoun with another school. At first I had been troubled that the other team was competing barefoot and that our boys, all wearing proper footgear, had an unfair advantage. However, the competent showing the visitors made in the opening events had diluted my concern. After all, I reasoned, the meet was taking place on grass, not the cinder runways I was used to, and those unshod youngsters seemed at home on the thick turf.

Suddenly Hahn was on the scene, talking with the visitors. He came over to me and said, "Those boys can't afford track shoes. Have our lads take off theirs and start the meet over." "But—." The decisiveness in his eyes stopped me. We started again, the meet now more closely contested. It took a long time for me to absorb fully the meaning of that incident. The lesson of fairness was clear enough. Still, no one would have thought it unfair if the headmaster had decided the only expedient was for our team to go barefoot in the remaining events. But in matters of fairness it was not Hahn's habit to consider expedience. In time I came to realize that the heart of the incident was his instant, uncompromising doing of what he knew to be right.

The Break, offering each an opportunity to build a base for his self-esteem, was a strong antidote to the campus sports-hero syndrome. So were the samaritan services—the Cliff Watchers, the Fire Service, and a little later, the Mountain Rescue team—and the school's mountain and sea expeditions. So were the Saturday mornings devoted to crafts; likewise a long-term project that each student worked on. The project might involve a craft, but it could be in nature, science, the arts, or some other area of student interest. The chief requirement was that it demand a sustained effort.

Hahn's zeal for the educational value of the crafts is especially memorable. His chief motivation was a deep respect for craftsmanship as a social force. The decline in skill and care, a major count in his indictment of the times, was "due to the weakened tradition of craftsmanship."

Perhaps the finest of his education stratagems was his use of the sea as a classroom. In nearby Hopeman Harbor, all Gordonstoun boys mastered small-boat seamanship and qualified to crew the *Prince Louis,* the school's seagoing sailing vessel. Again this was training not *for* but *through* the sea. Hahn said, "My best schoolmaster is the Moray Firth." It was Henry Brereton, scholar, historian, striver for academic excellence, who perceived that in that challenging body of water, with its strong tides, frequent high winds, and rocky shore, the elements were strict teachers of the values of discipline, order, skill—and of mathematics, learned as a tool of navigation. At the end of one holiday time the *Prince Louis* came back from a harrowing sea voyage around the Orkney and Shetland Islands having weathered three gales. Hahn asked a boy, "How did you enjoy yourself?" The boy said, "Magnificently, sir—except at the time." That became one of the headmaster's favorite stories, for it so beautifully supported his thesis that young people should be impelled into experience.

"Hahn's educational actions," noted an admiring German educator, "seem always to stem from two poles—justice and love. Should these ever be in conflict, then love conquers." He could, however, be very stern. The finer the boy being judged, the sterner the judgment. He was most demanding of the school's leaders; a leader had not only to earn his way to leadership but also his right to stay there. We had a youngster at Gordonstoun whose antisocial behavior—due apparently to a severe childhood trauma suffered during the war—became so bad that the school could not keep him. After much effort, Hahn found another school willing to take this boy. In a fury of spite on the day he was to leave, the boy made a shambles of his dormitory. When his housemates discovered the havoc, a group grabbed him arm and leg and started for the pond at the far end of the south lawn. The pond underlay the school's ropes course, and there was a rule that if you fell into its stagnant water, you had to be dosed with castor oil to purge tadpoles and other organisms you might have swallowed.

The Guardian, the school's student leader, was at some distance talking with companions when he saw what was happening. He watched as he continued talking. When, in a burst of decision, he raced to break up the kangaroo court, he was too late. By the time he reached the group, the boy had got his dunking and was suffering, if not a fit, a severe reaction. Under the Gordonstoun code, if a punishable offense took place in the Guardian's presence, only he was punished. I was astonished at the severity of Hahn's penalty. He not only relieved the Guardian of his post of leadership, he took away his Training Plan. What was most arresting was the reason for the penalty. The boy was not punished for his failure to prevent the dunking. His offense, said the bulletin board notice, was that he had hesitated before acting.

I used to tell that story but had to stop because I found it angered people. There would be murmurings: "Why, of course he hesitated. Any normal person would." Not in Hahn's book. In any moral crisis, he believed, a leader could hardly fail more grievously than not to know immediately what he should do, and promptly do it.

Hahn was an intrepid traveler; a journey with him was exhilarating. To see him cope with the usual frustrations of getting from one place to the next was to observe in microcosm ways in which he advanced his grand designs. Henry Brereton, who accompanied him on trips to Germany in the difficult travel years right after the war, has provided a lovely reminiscence: "Timetables seem to adjust to his whim, engine-drivers are in league with him and hold up the start of the express whilst he conducts an excited invalid infinitely slowly to her reserved compartment, saying with irritating assurance as guards blow whistles and porters shout and safely seated travelers stare from the windows, 'We have plenty of time, my dear. Don't hurry. There's plenty of time.'"

Brereton's vignette catches Hahn in a moment that, in its small but touching way, reflects the very heart of his personal philosophy. That was his profound commitment to the samaritan ethic. He had one hero above all: the compassionate traveler on the road to Jericho. Again and again he called for the Parable of the Good Samaritan to be read to the school. In the years to come I was to witness the growing power of his ultimate conviction—that through help to those "in danger and in need" youth can strike the deepest chords of the human spirit. It would become a creed: "He who drills and labors, accepts hardship, boredom, and dangers, all for the sake of helping his brother in peril and distress, discovers God's purpose in his inner life."

The summer of 1952 approached, when our time at Gordonstoun would be up. The matter of what I would do on our return to the States was of growing concern. In May, I was offered a teaching job at

Phillips Academy in Andover, Massachusetts, and decided to accept. Soon the day came for leave-taking. Hahn stood by the car with his gentle smile, bidding our family good-bye. "Look back over your left shoulder, but only once," he said. "Then you will surely return." When down the road we took that last look, the man who had changed my life forever was still standing with his hand raised in farewell. Turning back to the view of the road ahead, I made a promise to myself. I was resolved to help bring some aspect of his work to the United States.

This chapter was excerpted from *Outward Bound USA*, written by Joshua Miner and Joe Boldt, published by William Morris and Company, 1981.

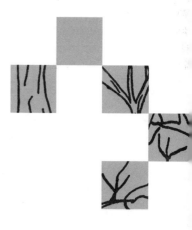

Demanding Much from the Young

Kurt Hahn

The following is an excerpt of a speech entitled "Training for and through the Sea," that Kurt Hahn gave in Glasgow, Scotland, on February 20, 1947.

I bring two accusations against our system. It fails to equip the average boy with a willing body. The gifted athlete is splendidly trained in our schools; the physical dunce, the sensitive and hesitant child are neglected in their physical education.…

On the strength of my twenty-seven years experience I do not hesitate to say: you can turn every normal boy into an athlete good enough to draw self-respect and self-confidence from his performances. You can do so on one condition: that you interrupt the sedentary habits of the morning by a training of at least forty-five minutes, in which a boy's resilience, his power of acceleration and co-ordination, his stamina are carefully exercised. The clumsy or timid boy soon will be fascinated by his unexpected progress. The ambition will grip him to train himself into a jumper, runner, and thrower capable of achieving certain standards. As a result, the spirit of adventure will be revived in those who had already resigned themselves to their physical inadequacy, and given up the dreams of their childhood.

My second accusation against our system of education is this: it fails to introduce activities into a boy's life like to make him discover his powers as a man of action.

At the beginning of this war, we experienced a remarkable change in the young. Every ounce of their human strength was claimed; the light of enterprise and daring was lit in their faces, and some of these young soldiers confessed to me that they felt a great release form their former existence, "which hardly could be called life."

I refuse to arrange a world war in every generation to rescue the young from a depressing peace. Let us rather plan their life at school so that they can discover and test their hidden powers. Education has no nobler task that to provide "the moral equivalent to war," as L. P. Jacks has told us twenty-five years ago. That this task can be fulfilled, nobody will doubt who has seen the triumph of mastery in a boy's face when he is conquering adversities on a sailing or mountaineering expedition. The present Headmaster of Eton has called such victories, "conquests without the humiliation of the conquered."

I have often shown the Gordonstoun (or Salem) Final Report form to teachers at Secondary Schools [see page 15]. Invariably I am told with a shrug of the shoulders: How can we recognize these traits of character within the curriculum laid down for our schools. My reply is: you cannot; unless you revolutionize your timetable to contain activities which reveal, test, and train character and in which you and your colleagues take an active part.

I recommend that training under sail or training in mountain craft be recognized as character-building activities good for the future worker, soldier, clerk, scholar, business man, lawyer or doctor. I may mention, here, that formerly the famous banking house of Wallenberg demanded that their future partners were trained at sea.

Inland schools should combine to have a training home on the hills or at the sea, in which short courses are held, modeled on the example of the Outward Bound Sea School. I also plead that more schools are planted near the sea.

A National Trust tenderly watches over castles and churches of the past. There is no more sacred treasure of a nation than the human nature of its citizens. We are not protecting this treasure against decay.

It is our educational system that is failing in this duty at protection, wasting the unique opportunities with which this island is blessed.

He who demands much from the young commands their willing service.

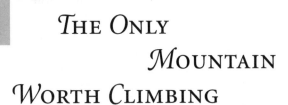

The Only Mountain Worth Climbing

An Historical and Philosophical Exploration of Outward Bound and Its Link to Education

Thomas James

Thomas James is vice dean and professor of Educational History in the School of Education at New York University. James has written about Kurt Hahn and the history of Outward Bound in a number of articles and publications, including the book Education at the Edge: The Colorado Outward Bound School. *He has also written essays on adventure and service in education.*

Outward Bound is more than a set of methods and activities. It represents a core of values, a philosophy of education. In this broader sense, as well as in its applications as a specific method of learning, Outward Bound has a deep historical affinity with conventional schooling.

The historical background is useful to consider when trying to understand the power of Outward Bound for improving schooling processes today. The moving spirit of Outward Bound, Kurt Hahn, employed challenge and outdoor adventure not for their own sake, but as a way of teaching perseverance, skill, teamwork, leadership, and compassionate service to the students at Gordonstoun, the school he founded in the 1930s. Having provided equipment and training, Hahn then established watch patrols for emergencies along the Scottish coast using teams of the privileged students from his high school. Hahn also decided to include other children from poor families living near Gordonstoun. He created a sense of moral community around demanding personal commitments to such things as fitness, craftsmanship, and service. He later widened this program into more systematic proposals such as the County Badge Scheme, Outward Bound, and the Duke of Edinburgh Award. Hahn's inclusion of poor children along with the rich established a cardinal principle that became part of Outward Bound in later years: bring together people from different social classes in common pursuits leading to self-discovery and service to others.

With the coming of World War II, Kurt Hahn became aware of the devastating toll that German submarines were taking on British ships in the North Sea. Building upon his experience as an educator who had used challenging outdoor activities requiring cooperation and craftsmanship along with academic learning, he and others devised a program of intensive training from initiatives he had been running at this school. The program became Outward Bound, which took its name from the nautical term for a ship leaving port on a sea journey.

Outward Bound developed into a separate organization during the war and eventually became a worldwide movement in its own right, resulting in several dozen schools all over the world. But it is significant that the program first took shape, pedagogically, as an educational innovation arising from a secondary school.

To understand the potential of Outward Bound for helping teachers and learners in schools, it is useful to look more closely at Hahn's educational values. This chapter considers Hahn the educator, the roots of his educational vision, and the relevance of his ideas to classrooms and schools today.

Let us begin by looking more closely at Kurt Hahn's life and times. Born in 1886, Hahn was the second of four sons in a Jewish family in Berlin. Schooled with conventional German rigor at the Wilhelms gymnasium, he graduated in 1904, the year in which he experienced a sunstroke that left him with a recurring disability for the rest of his life. Hahn went on to Oxford from 1904 to 1906 to read classics, with the support of his father, Oskar Hahn, industrialist and Anglophile. From 1906 to 1910, he studied at various universities—without, however, completing any degree. Returning to England in 1910, he continued to study at Oxford, and convalesced during the summers at Moray in northeastern Scotland, until the beginning of the Great War in 1914 called him home to Germany. Kurt Hahn never achieved a degree beyond his secondary schooling.

During the war, Hahn served as a reader for the German Foreign Office and then the Supreme Command, reviewing English-language newspapers to gauge popular opinion. Politically, he allied himself with those inside the German government who were seeking a negotiated peace in Western Europe instead of protracted war. Perceived as a liberal within the political spectrum of his day, Hahn advocated greater restraint in pushing German war aims. He espoused a code of responsibility that would be equally binding in war and peace; he used his influence behind the scenes to remind those in power about conciliatory factions at work within the governments of enemy nations.

At the end of the war, Prince Max von Baden asked Hahn to become his personal secretary. An articulate and enterprising young man, Hahn helped Prince Max, Germany's last imperial chancellor, to complete his memoirs, probably writing as much as editing. Whatever the form of their collaboration, the two men left a record of tough-minded idealism and political vigilance. When Prince Max returned to spend his last years at the ancestral castle of his family at Schloss Salem, by Lake Constance, he took Kurt Hahn with him and they discussed projects to renew the ethical traditions of German social life, traditions they believed were threatened not only by extremism on the right and left, but by incomprehension, moral failings, and lack of will in the middle. In 1920, with Prince Max as benefactor, Hahn opened Salem School in part of the castle.

Salem School, which still operates today, was influenced by the educational ideas of Plato, Cecil Reddie's Abbotsholme and other English schools started by German educators under the leadership of Herman Lietz. Salem represented an attempt to create a healthy environment in which young people could learn habits of life that would protect them against what Hahn saw as the deteriorating values of modern life. He identified the worst declines as those in fitness, memory and imagination, and compassion.

Directing the school from 1920 until 1933, Hahn placed greater emphasis on noncompetitive physical activities and democratic forms of social cooperation than was the case in conventional German schools. At the urging of Prince Max, he incorporated egalitarian aims into the design of the school; while Salem naturally attracted the children of the wealthy, it also made space for, and actively sought, less privileged students. Emulating the Cistercian monks who had inhabited the castle for many centuries, the students and teachers at Salem School helped the surrounding communities through various forms of service, including a fire brigade.

The curriculum at Salem prepared young people for higher education, but not without laying the groundwork for a life of moral and civic virtue, the chief aims of the school. Among the unusual assumptions underlying all forms of instruction at Salem was Hahn's conviction that students should experience failure as well as success. They should learn to overcome negative inclinations within themselves and prevail against all adversity.

He believed, moreover, that students should learn to discipline their own needs and desires for the good of the community. They should realize through their own experience the connection between self-discovery and service. He also insisted that true learning required periods of silence and solitude as well as directed activity. Each day the students took a silent walk to commune with nature and revitalize their powers of reflection.

To keep mental and physical growth in balance, Hahn developed the notion of a training plan for his students, each of whom committed himself to an individually designed, gradually more challenging regimen of physical exercise and personal hygiene. Unlike the physical education program of other schools, the aim of the training plan was simply to establish good living habits, not to produce high levels of performance in competitive games.

An assassin failed to end Hahn's life in 1923. Still in his early thirties, the schoolmaster was controversial, a gadfly, a target because he was a moral leader far beyond the lives of his students and teachers. The director of Salem—the school's name means peace—idolized few men in his lifetime, but one incident he often recounted was the confrontation between Max Weber, Germany's most distinguished social scientist, and an angry crowd of leftist demonstrators in 1918. Weber shouted that he had never crawled before kings and emperors in the past, and he was not going to crawl before any mob now.

Similarly, Kurt Hahn refused to back down from the moral aims that animated every aspect of education as far as he was concerned. In a nation frighteningly polarized by the right and the left in political debate, Hahn forced educational issues into the larger discussion of how society should be organized, and what people must do to maintain human decency in a world of conflict. No idyllic schoolmaster's life awaited him.

When it finally came, in the early 1930s, the controversy that pushed Kurt Hahn out of Germany involved the right, not the left. As the Nazis rose to power, the director of Salem School became an outspoken opponent. In 1932 a group of fascist storm troopers kicked a leftist activist to death before the eyes of his mother. Adolph Hitler immediately praised the action of his followers. Kurt Hahn wrote to the alumni of Salem, telling them to choose between Salem and Hitler. A man who knew Hahn at the time called it "the bravest deed in cold blood that I have ever witnessed." When he became chief of state in 1933, Hitler imprisoned Hahn. Fortunately for the embattled educator, he still had friends in Britain who remembered his idealism and his hopes for friendship between the two nations. Prime Minister Ramsay MacDonald and others helped to arrange for Hahn's release and timely emigration to England in 1933.

Within a year of his arrival, Kurt Hahn started another institution, Gordonstoun, which became one of Britain's most distinguished progressive schools and served as a model for similar schools in other countries. In the following decades, Hahn's educational vision served as the moving spirit for new institutions and programs of worldwide renown: the Moray Badge and County Badge Schemes and their successor, the Duke of Edinburgh Awards; Outward Bound; the Trevelyan Scholarships; and the United World Colleges.

Reaching back into this pre-history of Outward Bound, we might well look for the origins of the idea in 1913 instead of 1941, when Outward Bound was founded. For in the summer of 1913, instead of vacationing, as he hoped, with a friend in Scotland, and while recuperating from the sunstroke he had suffered a few years before, Kurt Hahn outlined his idea for a school based on principles set forth in Plato's *Republic*. Hahn was 28 years old and had never run a school, or even taught in one. The ideal school he imagined never came into being, but it exerted a profound influence on all his subsequent efforts as an educator and statesman: Salem School, in Germany, in 1920; Gordonstoun School, in Scotland, in 1934; Outward Bound in Wales, in 1941; and Atlantic College, in England, in 1962.

In *English Progressive Schools,* Robert Skidelsky analyzes Hahn's debt to Plato as follows:

> Plato was a political reformer who sought to
> recall the Athenians to the old civic virtues

eroded, as he saw it, by democratic enthusiasm and soft living. His aim was to educate a class of leaders in a "healthy pasture" remote from the corrupting environment, whose task it would be to regenerate society. Hahn must have been haunted by similar visions of decay as, inspired by these ideas, he drew up a plan in 1913 for a school modeled on Platonic principles. The war that broke out a year later and ended in the collapse of Germany was to give them a new urgency: to convert what might have remained a purely academic speculation into an active campaign for social and political regeneration.

Outward Bound places unusual emphasis on physical challenge, not as an end in itself, but as an instrument for training the will to strive for mastery. There is also the insistent use of action, instead of states of mind, to describe the reality of the individual. Education is tied unequivocally to experience, to what one does and not so much to one's attitudes and opinions.

A thread running from Plato through Hahn and through Outward Bound is the responsibility of individuals to make their own personal goals consonant with social necessity. Not only is the part subordinated to the whole, but the part cannot even understand its own identity, its relations and its responsibility, until it has grasped the nature of the whole. Having stood up to Hitler before being exiled from Nazi Germany in 1933, Hahn believed in individual freedom, but he believed that students should be impelled into experiences that would teach them the bonds of social life necessary to protect such freedom. He took from Plato the idea that a human being cannot achieve perfection without becoming part of a perfect society—that is, without creating social harmony to sustain the harmonious life of the individual.

This is the overall structure of the argument in the *Republic,* and it is also the most important lesson of an Outward Bound course, the lesson without which personal development is of questionable value. In a small group away from the degenerate ways of the world, the individual student comes to grips with what must be done to create a just society. In attempting to construct such a challenge, Hahn placed compassion above all other values of Outward Bound because it, among all emotions, is capable of reconciling individual strength with collective need.

The prospect of wholeness, the possibility, at least, of human life becoming an equilibrium sustained by harmony and balance, is what makes this form of education even thinkable. Skidelsky again offers a lucid analysis of the source of Hahn's thinking:

> The second idea which Hahn assimilated was
> Plato's notion that the principle of perfection

was harmony and balance. The perfection of the body, he held, depends upon a harmony of its elements. Virtue (the health of the soul) is the harmony or balance between the various faculties of the psyche: reason, the appetites and spirit.

Virtue in the state is the harmony between its functional elements: thinkers, soldiers and artisans. The same principle can be extended indefinitely—to relations between states, and so on.

This passage sheds some light on Hahn's interest in giving his students experiences that would complement their strengths and weaknesses. In his speeches he said he wanted to turn introverts inside out and extroverts outside in. He wanted the poor to help the rich break their "enervating sense of privilege" and the rich to help the poor in building a true "aristocracy of talent."

The schools he founded sent bookworms to the playing fields and jocks to the reading room. He did not produce outstanding athletes, but his students exhibited consistently high levels of fitness, accomplishment and social spirit. He said he valued mastery in the sphere of one's weakness over performance in the sphere of one's strength.

The preceding paragraphs do not record Hahn's debt to other thinkers, such as Rousseau, Goethe and William James, to name a few. William James, for example, in his "The Moral Equivalent of War," asked if it is not possible in time of peace to build the kind of social spirit and productivity one takes for granted in time of war. Hahn saw Outward Bound as an answer to that question. Goethe wrote of an education that would need to occur in a place apart, a "Pedagogical Province," so that individuals could be strengthened and given skills to survive, individually and collectively, in the debilitating environment of human society as we know it. Hahn was indebted to Rousseau, both for the idea that awakening an individual's collective concern is the key to healthy personal development and also for Rousseau's assumption that Nature is an educator in its own right, more akin to the true nature of a human being than is the society that humans have built for themselves.

Hahn remarked once that we in the Western world are confronted by a progressive inhumanity of the society in which we live. He said that he saw Outward Bound as a countervailing force against the decline of initiative due, in his words, to the widespread disease of "spectatoritis," the decline of skill and care due to the weakening traditions of craftsmanship, and the decline of concern about one's neighbor due to the unseemly haste with which daily life is conducted. In 1930, three years before his exile from Germany for opposing Hitler, he drew up "The Seven Laws of Salem" to describe his educational methods.

First Law

"GIVE CHILDREN THE OPPORTUNITY FOR
SELF-DISCOVERY.

Every boy and girl has *grande passion,* often hidden
and unrealized to the end of life. The educator cannot
hope and may not try to find it out by psychoanalytical
methods. It can and will be revealed by the child
coming into close touch with a number of different
activities. When a child has come 'into his own,' you
will often hear a shout of joy, or be thrilled by some
other manifestation of primitive happiness."

Second Law

"MAKE THE CHILDREN MEET WITH TRIUMPH
AND DEFEAT.

It is possible to wait on a child's inclinations and
gifts and to arrange carefully for an unbroken series
of successes. You may make him happy in this way—
I doubt it—but you certainly disqualify him for the
battle of life. Salem believes you ought to discover
the child's weakness as well as his strength. Allow
him to engage in enterprises in which he is likely to
fail, and do not hush up his failure. Teach him to
overcome defeat."

Third Law

"GIVE THE CHILDREN THE OPPORTUNITY OF
SELF-EFFACEMENT IN THE COMMON CAUSE.
Send the youngsters out to undertake tasks which are

of definite importance for the community. Tell them from the start: 'You are a crew, not passengers. Let the responsible boys and girls shoulder duties big enough, when negligently performed, to wreck the State.'"

Fourth Law

"PROVIDE PERIODS OF SILENCE.
Follow the great precedent of the Quakers. Unless the present-day generation acquires early habits of quiet and reflection, it will be speedily and prematurely used up by the nerve-exhausting and distracting civilization of today."

Fifth Law

"TRAIN THE IMAGINATION.
You must call it into action, otherwise it becomes atrophied like a muscle not in use. The power to resist the pressing stimulus of the hour and the moment cannot be acquired in later life; it often depends on the ability to visualize what you plan and hope and fear for the future. Self-indulgence is in many cases due to the lack of vision."

Sixth Law

"MAKE GAMES (I.E., COMPETITION) IMPORTANT
BUT NOT PREDOMINANT.
Athletes don't suffer by being put in their place.
In fact you restore the dignity of the usurper by dethroning him."

SEVENTH LAW

"FREE THE SONS OF THE WEALTHY AND
POWERFUL FROM THE ENERVATING SENSE
OF PRIVILEGE.
Let them share the experiences of an enthralling school
life with sons and daughters of those who have to
struggle for their existence. No school can build up a
tradition of self-discipline and vigorous but joyous
endeavor unless at least 30 percent of the children come
from homes where life is not only simple but hard."

Writing in 1941, Hahn listed the benefits that such
an education offered the individual student: "He will
have a trained heart and a trained nervous system
which will stand him in good stead in fever, exposure
and shock; he will have acquired spring and powers
of acceleration; he will have built up stamina and
know how to tap his hidden resources. He may enjoy
the well-being which goes with a willing body. He
will have trained his tenacity and patience, his
initiative and forethought, his power of observation
and his power of care. He will have developed
steadfastness and he will be able to say 'No' to the
whims of the moment. He will have stimulated and
nourished health interests until they become lively
and deep, and perhaps develop into a passion. The
average boy when first confronted with these tests
will nearly always find some which look forbidding,
almost hopelessly out of his reach; others he will find

easy and appealing to his innate strength; but once he has started training he will be gripped by magic—a very simple magic, the magic of the puzzle... and he will struggle on against odds until one day he is winning through in spite of some disability. There always is some disability; but in the end he will triumph, turning defeat into victory, thus overcoming his own defeatism."

Kurt Hahn brought intensity to Outward Bound by asking difficult questions: "Can a demanding active service to their fellow man, in need and in danger, become an absorbing leisure activity for an ever-increasing number of young people?" And he came up with difficult answers: "We need an aristocracy of service as an example to inspire others to do likewise."

Hahn said he wanted to introduce into the art of life-saving the meticulous care which is generally devoted to the art of war, and he quoted William James to the effect that inspiration tends to evaporate, leaving no trace on future conduct, unless it is translated into action. He suggested to Outward Bound that the secret of education was to teach young people the inner strength that comes from serving others. "There are three ways to win the young. There's persuasion, there is compulsion and there is attraction. You can preach at them: that is the hook without the worm; you can order them to volunteer: that is dishonest; you can call on them, *'you are needed,'* and that appeal hardly ever fails." He reasoned that "the experience of helping a fellow man in danger, or even of training in a realistic manner to be ready to give his help, tends to change the balance of power in a youth's inner life with the result that compassion can become the master motive."

Not long after leaving prison in Germany and just after founding Gordonstoun in Scotland, Hahn described the three essential approaches to education that he saw about him. He called them the Ionian, the Spartan and the Platonic. "The first believes that the individual ought be nurtured and humored, regardless of the interests of the community. According to the second, the individual may and should be neglected for the benefit of the state. The third, the Platonic view, believes that any nation is a slovenly guardian of its own interests if it does not do all it can to make the individual citizen discover his own powers. And it further believes that the individual becomes a cripple from his or her own point of view if he is not qualified by education to serve the community."

In school, Hahn asked his students to pledge themselves to the "training plan," establishing personal goals and a code of responsibility. Outward Bound instructors make a similar appeal to their students today, though not in the detailed terms used by Hahn at Salem and Gordonstoun, and it is a crucial aspect of the Outward Bound experience. The individual commitment of the student, the expressed desire to accomplish a worthy goal by means of the course, becomes, in effect, the moral basis of the community, the foundation both of compassion and of achievement.

Another important element that Hahn brought to Outward Bound was adventure—with all the risk it entails. He believed that education should cultivate a passion for life and that this can be accomplished only through experience, a shared sense of moment in the journey toward an exciting goal. Mountaineering and sailing were integral parts of his program at Gordonstoun, and he made space in all his programs for student initiative—an expedition, a project, a sailing voyage. Hahn welcomed powerful emotions, such as awe, fear, exultant triumph. Part of his lifelong aspiration, part of the "whole" he sought through programs like Outward Bound, was that the experience accessible to any human being, at any level of ability, could be charged with joy and wonder in the doing.

Hahn also understood the educational value of working with small groups of students. He probably took this idea from military organization as it came into the youth movements of the late 19th century, especially the Scouting movement of Lord Baden-Powell in England. Hahn saw small groups as a way to develop natural leadership abilities he thought were present in most people, but such an inquiry would eventually miss the point. They were suppressed by the dependency, passivity, and bureaucratic impersonality of modern life. Such groups place heavy social pressures on individual initiative, yet at the same time they require it absolutely. Small groups require tremendous amounts of energy to reach the consensus necessary to meet objectives. Natural leaders emerge when a group must solve real problems instead of playing games with an unnatural reward system. A genuine community begins to appear on a small scale.

A concern encompassing all the rest was Hahn's dedication to community service. As Hahn saw it, the link between individual and school depended for its meaning upon the link between school and society. The notion came into Outward Bound in the form of rescue service, and it has since been applied to diverse needs in communities and the natural environment.

With such distinctive origins, it is only natural that Outward Bound should seek to ally itself more closely with conventional schooling. As the Outward Bound movement expanded after World War II, it was carried into the United States initially by educators such as Joshua L. Miner of Phillips Academy, Andover, and F. Charles Froelicher of Colorado Academy. From the 1960s through the 1970s, Outward Bound sought as an explicit aim to influence American schooling by persuading teachers and administrators to adapt experiential methods from the outdoor program to enhance formal learning.

The aim was not to manage such projects. Outward Bound turned over its ideas to school personnel for development within the schools, both public and private. For example, the Outward Bound schools set up teachers' courses and attempted to transmit ideals and methods in order to make an imprint on the dominant pattern of schooling for adolescents. The responses of participants from conventional schools emphasized the pedagogical vitality of experiential methods as well as the team building and depth of mutual commitment elicited from students on Outward Bound courses. Studies of in-school adaptations produced some alternative models and promising but ambiguous results.

Beginning in the early 1970s, Project Adventure, an offshoot of Outward Bound started by instructors wishing to work more closely with conventional schools, achieved success in applying experiential methods derived from Outward Bound to the schools. Project Adventure, which has been identified as an exemplary model by the National Diffusion Program of the U. S. Department of Education, went on to develop a repertoire of its own, paralleled by other creative offshoot programs, to assist in adventure programming, teacher training, and counseling.

By the mid-1970s, Outward Bound was part of a larger movement in the United States, referred to broadly as experiential education. The movement had some impact through generating alternative programs for adaptation by public and private schools, including not only outdoor education but such widely implemented strategies as action learning, experience-based career education, and cultural journalism. But while it had philo-sophical roots in common with these innovations, Outward Bound pursued a strategy of staying apart organizationally, mostly offering ideas and short-term training, then hoping that mainstream institutions would replicate what might prove most effective.

In the remainder of this chapter I would like to offer a personal interpretation of Kurt Hahn's vision of learning, one that attempts to connect the events

of his life with his ideas. I believe it is this vision of
Hahn's that shows most clearly what Outward Bound
has to offer American education.

Kurt Hahn understood weakness better than
strength. The goal of learning, in his view, was
compensatory: to purify the destructive inclinations
of the human personality, to redress the imbalances
in modern ways of living, to develop each person's
disabilities to their maximum potential, and to place
new-found strength in service of those in need. Kurt
Hahn was suspicious of presumed excellence; he
paid scant attention to the glories of unsurpassed
individual performance, whether it be on the playing
fields at Eton or the examination ordeal of the German
gymnasium. He understood, as few educators have so
well, the tender fears of young people, their alienation
before the rigors and rituals of adult power. He
understood how wrong it was to vanquish them with
that power to make them learn. This strategy would
only deepen their confusion about the meaning of
their lives, making them cynical, lacking in humanity,
even if it strengthened them. Hahn's favorite story was
the Good Samaritan, wherein the strong, those clearly
in a position to help the most, failed to act. It was the
outsider, the weak, the despised who taught what it
means to be a civilized human being.

Where did Hahn learn this, and if he once felt it
himself, how did he convert his own weakness into
an enduring vision of education? We must look, I
believe, to the most tumultuous time of life to see the
emerging center. In late adolescence, on the threshold

of higher education and adult life, Hahn felt the impact of three events that changed his life.

The first was an expedition, some days of fresh air and majestic surroundings on a walking tour of the Dolomite Alps. One can well imagine the exhilaration of a boy in his teens on such a rite of passage. Famed for their bold, other-worldly shapes, their awe-inspiring hues of light and shadow from sunrise to sunset, the Dolomites imprinted on Hahn an inextinguishable love of natural beauty. As an educator, he would always be devising ways to turn his classrooms out of doors, putting his students into motion and forcing his teachers to come to grips with the healing powers of direct experience.

But something else happened on this expedition. A second event added to these other feelings a specific passion, strong enough to organize his self-discovery into a lifelong vocation. Two English schoolboys who accompanied Hahn gave him a gift, a book called *Emlohstobba* by the German educator Herman Lietz. The title of the book was the name of their school, Abbotsholme, spelled backwards. Lietz wrote rapturously of life inside that school, where he served as master of studies for a sabbatical year under the innovative headmaster, Cecil Reddie. When Lietz returned to Germany, he fathered the country school movement there, inspiring others to begin schools more healthful for young people than the prevailing system of the time.

For Hahn this book was a momentous gift. Along with the living example of the two students from Abbotsholme, who impressed him with their healthy love of life, and the sheer beauty of their alpine journey together, young Hahn must have felt in himself a new conviction of life's possibilities. Coming at a time when his own formal education was marching lockstep through the authoritarian, rigidly academic curriculum of the gymnasium, the alternative vision of a more humane and democratic school, capable of fostering more perfect human beings, seized his imagination with a force that can be judged only by abandoning strict chronology and looking ahead to the seventy indefatigable years of institution-building that lay ahead of him.

It was not on that trip, however, that Hahn imagined the school he hoped to build. Two years later, the year of his graduation from the gymnasium, a third event completed his initiation. He suffered the life-threatening sunstroke that permanently changed his life. Never again would he have the freedom to trek or sail long pleasurable distances out of doors. Nor was it certain, in the weeks following the accident, whether he would recover enough to participate in normal functions of life. Depression set in, squelching his hopes. One would not be surprised if his boyhood dreams became cruel reminders of all that was not possible now. His life was a washout, a failure before it had really begun.

Here, and not in his later life of so many memorable accomplishments, the educational genius of the man is to be found. The center emerged as a discovery of who he really was inside, the gift of suddenly knowing what he had to do, and would do, when he bumped up against his own limitations. It was the scale of values, the plan of life, the desired future he asserted as his response to adversity when it came.

Adversity came to Hahn in several forms, all of which must have seemed insuperable from his perspective in a darkened room as he recovered from his accident. The physical disability would always be present in his life. It would be necessary for him to wear a broad-brimmed hat to protect his head from the sunlight. Frail in the heat, he would have to flee northward to a cooler climate for the summers. Periodically, he would need to undergo major operations to relieve the fluid pressure within his head. All this he knew, or could well imagine, in those months of convalescence.

In his darkened room, Kurt Hahn regenerated his spirit with a vision of what he could do with his life. He decided that he would someday start a school modeled on principles drawn from Plato's *Republic,* a school that would expand the wholesome influence he identified with Herman Lietz and Cecil Reddie's Abbotsholme. How much of the vision came to him at that time and how much later is not clear, but he grasped the essential outline. The school would harmonize the social and intellectual differences between its students by operating as a community of participation and active service. It would seek out the natural qualities of leadership, skill, and responsibility possessed by all in different ways when they see that they are truly needed. His school of the future would harmonize the wild and discordant personality of the adolescent by demonstrating that true need.

Once again, it is difficult to say how much of that vision became evident to Hahn during his recovery and how much came to him as glimpses and inklings which he later converted into plans and traditions. That the center emerged, though, is indisputable, both by his own account and because of the central place he gave to his thoughts during the dark night of the soul in later educational projects.

How could his vision be made believable to the alienated young? Closer to home, how could Kurt Hahn himself, in his debility and depression, bring himself to believe in a better life? Forced by the accident to reflect upon his own childhood, to seek out some deeper matrix of meaning to keep his spirits up, Hahn came face to face with his own youthful passion. That there exists, in everyone, a grand passion, an outlandish thirst for adventure, a desire to live boldly and vividly in the journey through life, sprang forth as the most salient lesson of his lifelong pedagogy.

That was not all, however, and it was not enough. For now the Dolomites and the classics flowed together to become Hahn's vision of the good. Dwelling for a time in his imagined world of Plato as he dreamed of a future school, and feeling his spirit awakening to a great sense of purpose in that semi-darkness after the sunstroke, Hahn made the crucial connection. Passion must not be treated lightly. Its deep springs in human nature must not be poisoned. Above all, it must not be misdirected and turned to inhumane ends. The grand passion of the young must be embraced in wholesome ways by adult power. It must be nurtured instead of deformed or punished. Its creative force must be harnessed to the quest for a good society, the aim of Plato's educational designs. To accomplish this purpose would require more than a school in a traditional sense. Some separation from the existing human world, into the intensity of a journey-quest, confronting challenges and transforming opportunities for service, could change the balance of power in young people, Hahn believed. Then they would be more inclined to use their lives, back in the world from which they came, to bring the good society into being.

With the center in view, the chronology of Kurt Hahn's life takes on greater meaning. Expelled from the land of his birth, the schoolmaster continued his career in Britain, which became a second homeland for him. When he opened Gordonstoun in 1934, Hahn carried the Salem tradition to the new setting, and he brought staff and students with him. New features appeared, such as the addition of rescue training to the service program. And some of the old practices changed, or were presented differently, in response to the cultural milieu of the British Isles. All this, of course, is to be expected in transplanting the design of an institution from one place and time to another. Certainly the transition was made easier by the strong affinity of Hahn's thinking with the traditions of Abbotsholme and the English public schools. What stands out, nonetheless, is the fact that Hahn was able in so short a time to create a new institution which, like his first school, would become known around the world for its distinctive educational practices.

If Hahn had not been restless, if he had not felt driven toward wider applications of his principles beyond any school he might ever create, he would perhaps have settled in to a longer career as the eccentric headmaster of a school favored by the English aristocracy. But he was not satisfied. He began to organize a constellation of other education forms around Gordonstoun, using the school as a staging ground for programs through which he hoped to instruct the whole society around him in the first lessons of sound living and civic responsibility. The Moray Badge Scheme took form in 1936, followed quickly by the larger and better known County Badge a year later.

Along the way, Hahn experimented with short courses to discover the combination of challenging experiences that might help young people discover new ways of organizing their lives and working with other people. In 1941, with Laurence Holt, Hahn started Outward Bound as a short course. Initially, the goal was to strengthen the will of young men so that they could prevail against adversity as Great Britain faced staggering losses at sea during World War II. After the program had demonstrated its effectiveness, it continued to expand during the postwar years, furnishing opportunities for personal and social growth to many people beyond the original clientele of boys and young men.

Chronology alone cannot account for Hahn's widening sphere of educational activity. Only by grasping how he continued to draw both from a sense of weakness and from the strong idealism at the center of his being can we understand his intuitive leaps as he created new programs over the years. Hahn perceived clearly that schools as we know them are not equal to the urgent problem of social life in this century. Even the best schools probably damage as much as develop the volatile inner lives of young people.

One reason for this unintended consequence is that schools represent only a partial solution to a much more pervasive problem. The problem of how to educate the whole person cannot be resolved without learning how to civilize human communities, which in turn cannot be done without preparing the entire world society in the arts of living harmoniously at the highest levels of potential activity and understanding. Hahn's debt to Plato was his conviction that education must embrace all these aspects of human life. A vision of what is most desirable in education must embody not only some notion of how the whole is to be organized, but what it will take for that whole to be good. Without a vision of wholeness, without at least a hope that the compassionate community might someday be realized on a worldwide scale, people are not inclined to live on humane terms with one another.

Exiled to the British Isles, Kurt Hahn was restless at the center of his being. Carrying with him an unflinching impression of the expanding Third Reich and its effects on European civilization, he could never be satisfied with the auspicious beginning of a school. Soon after his arrival he began to write and speak in public, deploring the general lack of fitness among the British people. He urged his hosts to recognize the need for programs on a large scale that would combine individual training plans with group projects to build stronger civic consciousness.

Out of such concerns he initiated the Moray and County Badge Schemes. The latter quickly expanded and became further elaborated in many counties across the British Isles, spreading even to other countries in the British Commonwealth. The County Badge granted public recognition to young people who completed a planned course of challenges. They first adopted a training plan of physical conditioning and personal health habits. Then they undertook an arduous expedition requiring group decision-making as well as individual effort. They also completed a project demanding new skills and craftsmanship. Finally, they engaged in service activities, experiencing the value of compassion through direct action on behalf of the community or specific people in need.

At the beginning of the war, the County Badge contained most of the essential features of the Outward Bound program as it would develop in future years. Indeed, the secretary and key promoter of the County Badge Experimental Committee, James Hogan, became the first warden of the first Outward

Bound School at Aberdovey, in Wales. Yet there was a difference, and it was more than the residential setting and month-long sustained program of Outward Bound. Although both programs offered models for changing how individuals organized their lives, there was something more universal and enduring about Outward Bound.

Hahn had realized how close are weakness and strength in the most powerful forms of education. In his own day, he perceived clearly, while others did not, the subtle line that distinguishes compassionate service from destructive egotism. On the one hand, he feared the lack of will among those whose lives stood in the path of the advancing Third Reich. Hence his call for programs like the County Badge to build fitness and commit young people to civic ideas. But on the other hand, he recognized the affinity between his methods and those of the Nazis, one used for the good, the other for deadly ends.

There is an irony in this affinity, since Hahn was criticized by some in England for importing the paramilitary methods of the Hitler Youth. The irony is that the Hitler Youth movement did not discover the intensive methods of socialization they used to unleash the energies of the young. Rather, they borrowed from the leading educators of the day and applied the methods to their own goals. Hahn knew this well, for he had seen Hitler Youth before he left Germany. Their leaders had adapted and twisted to demonic purposes the training plan of Salem. Hahn had witnessed, therefore, the effects of reaching the whole person with the fascist plan of life instead of a Samaritan ethic. Hitler and his followers were reinforcing the passion of the young, giving them a spirit of adventure, introducing them to self-development and cooperation in the outdoors, then giving them meaningful opportunities to serve. Hahn recognized that there was no time for complacency. The weakness of the status quo must be acknowledged. All education must be made activist, or else the humane values upon which western democracies were built would succumb to a determined usurper.

Not even in its desperate beginnings before the onslaught of the Third Reich did Outward Bound ever train young people for war, but it arose fully conscious of the challenge presented by the Hitler Youth, that nationwide mobilization of young people to serve the cause of world conquest and genocide. Never did anyone press Outward Bound toward becoming a preparation for violence, and in this respect it would always remain distinct from youth mobilizations under totalitarian regimes. Yet it is difficult to imagine how Outward Bound would ever have come into being if it had not been for Hahn's recognition of the weakness of democratic cultures before well-organized forms of authoritarian education that were appallingly efficient at stirring up the passions of the young for collective violence.

Through Outward Bound, Hahn hoped to foster a deeper intensity of commitment in the rite of passage from youth to adult life. He was intent on creating more dramatic challenges and victories for the young than were available in conventional forms of schooling. Advocating a more arduous quest than was present in the institutions around him, Hahn was working from a disability greater than his own, a collective predicament verging on catastrophe. In England during the German Blitzkrieg, it was by no means apocalyptic to argue that there would need to be a new education, reconstructed on a massive scale, to produce the compassionate army needed to preserve what was left of civilization at home. Hahn believed that an intensive program of training, expedition, reflection and service would make a difference.

That belief survived beyond the exigencies of war, but Hahn's own direct role quickly receded once the philosophical values were in place to launch Outward Bound. While Hahn continued to influence Outward Bound, it soon took on a life of its own under the vigorous leadership of many people drawn to its idealism and hardy lifestyle over the years. Taking an image from Plato, Hahn likened himself to a midwife of educational projects as he sparked ideas for new endeavors and then left much of the development and maintenance to others. Outward Bound sea and mountain schools proliferated across several continents in the following decades. As it adapted itself to different cultures in later years, Outward Bound lost its wartime urgency, but it maintained a zest for adventure and Hahn's legacy of moral purpose.

Outward Bound has come to mean many things in different places and for the great variety of people who are drawn to it, but at its heart, in every time

and place, is Hahn's own center, his conviction
that it is possible, even in a relatively short time,
to introduce greater balance and compassion into
human lives by impelling people into experiences
which show them they can rise above adversity and
overcome their own defeatism, make more of their
lives than they thought they could, and learn to
serve others with their strength.

Hahn's postwar contributions include several
other projects of which he considered himself more
midwife than instigator. It would be most accurate to
characterize him as the moving spirit, since his arts of
persuasion were decisive in each case. The Trevelyan
Scholarships, for example, provided funds for young
people to attend Oxford and Cambridge Universities
based on experimental as well as academic criteria:
applicants were asked to complete a project of their
own design, which would be reviewed by a selection
panel. Shortly after a recurrence of his sunstroke in
the early 1950s, Hahn helped to launch the Duke of
Edinburgh Award, a program similar to the County
Badge but much more widely developed throughout
the British Commonwealth. His crowning achievement after the war was the United World Colleges,
which began with the founding of Atlantic College
in 1962.

If Outward Bound's origins are to be found in the
war, those of the United World Colleges appear in
the desire to build institutions that will offer a living
example of what it means to be at peace. Taking
students from 16 to 19, equivalent to the sixth form

in England or the last two years before postsecondary education in the United States, these colleges bring together boys and girls from all over the world, from competing social and economic systems, from rival cultures and religions. The program fosters world citizenship, an interconnected leadership of people who have experienced a collective life of active dialogue and peacemaking service. The curriculum, like that of Gordonstoun, combines both academic and experiential challenges, but the institutions have developed in new directions under their diverse leadership, leaving some of Hahn's educational practices behind while preserving others. Kurt Hahn's original insight that such institutions were possible stands as perhaps the greatest legacy of his influence as they continued to thrive and expand in the 1980s.

Returning to Germany for his last days, Kurt Hahn died near Salem, in Hermannsberg, on December 14, 1974. The entry in Britain's *Dictionary of National Biography* calls him "headmaster and citizen of humanity." Hahn's educational influence persists in such organizations as the Round Square Conference, comprised of schools modeled on Salem and Gordonstoun. His genius in devising short-term educational experiences has not stopped infusing energy and inspiration into the Outward Bound Trust, which oversees Outward Bound schools throughout the world. His love of peace flourishes in the United World Colleges, not to mention the many other institutions and individuals who continue to embody his ideals. This man's educational vision remains, beckoning like an adventure, arising from weakness to teach about strength, turning self-discovery into acts of compassion, everywhere defending human decency.

Reprinted with permission of the author and Outward Bound®, Inc. Material from this article was also included in the *Journal of Experiential Education, Into the Classroom,* and *Fieldwork: An Expeditionary Learning Outward Bound Reader, Volume I.*

THE MISSING DIMENSION

PAUL YLVISAKER

*A national leader in philanthropy, public policy, and
education, Paul Ylvisaker was at different times dean of
the Harvard University Graduate School of Education,
commissioner of Community Affairs for the State of
New Jersey, and director of National Affairs for the Ford
Foundation. Below is an excerpt of a keynote speech he
gave at the 1987 International Outward Bound
Conference in Cooperstown, New York.*

*L*et me detail five or six of what I see to be the
changes that education and all of us are trying to cope
with. First, there is in this century and in this world, an
exploding buildup of human power. It is a buildup
that is not fully released, and the only analogy that I
can give you to support this is that of the atomic pile.
We have put together a human atomic pile, in which
the atoms have been split and this fantastic power is
available, but if you don't put graphite rods in the
reactor and channel those energies, the pile will melt

down. When you take a look around the world today and you see these fantastic human energies that are available, you begin thinking, if only we could channel and give positive constructive release to this pile.

The second change is the basic shift in social concepts. We are moving away from the social stratification that has dominated the world's history with repressions, and are beginning to think of human beings each as ends in themselves. Remember Emmanual Kant saying that we should never—as a first imperative of behavior—treat human beings as means, but only as ends. If you read the ambitions and aspirations of the world today, you can feel the demand of human beings that they be regarded as ends.

The third change is that we have a dawning appreciation of what it means to be a whole person, not fragmented into pieces that can be exploited on an assembly line. We each, when born, have a chance to mold ourselves, to form ourselves into that human being which we and others respect. The fourth change is the growing recognition of what it takes for effective learning by a whole human being.

The fifth—and this is something I want to spend a little time with—is a growing appreciation and a premium placed on the mind. It used to be that in the more primary and secondary forms of the economy —mining, manufacturing, farming—that we used human bodies and muscles and only a few developed "the mind." Now, we recognize that we are in a society that is knowledge-based, and that we must perfect the development of the mind.

Finally we are beginning to form a new conception of the mind. We have been dominated for a century by the identification of the mind with the I.Q. Now we are beginning to see that there is something about the mind that defies that easy classification. A colleague of mine, Howard Gardner, has developed a book called *Frames of Mind*. He has identified seven distinct mental competencies. They include the linguistic, the logical, the musical, the spatial, and the kinesthetic. The final two competencies are what Gardner calls personal. One is the capacity for introspection. The other personal competency is the social—the capacity to empathize, to be able to read other people, and to fit in with them.

Notice that even Gardner's reconceptualization of the brain still talks about the brain. What you will not find in Gardner's book are two other qualities, the spiritual and the motivational. How do you get a person to begin wanting to use these competencies? That is where part of our educational system has come to a standstill.

EDUCATION TODAY

Take a look at education as we are now experiencing it. Even in our own domestic mood of reform in this last decade, we have concentrated on those competencies of the mind that are the conventional: reading, writing, working hard, going to school for a longer time like the Japanese, and all the rest of it. All of the reforms that legislatures and educators have been talking about have to do with curriculum and the conventions of the game. They have not gotten to some of these other qualities that we ought to be nourishing, nor have they talked about motivation or values during this period of time. The result has been, sometimes, a retrogression in the movement.

Another shortcoming of education today is the way the principle of exclusion wins out over inclusion. The downgrading of what we do with the disadvantaged population still is obvious in the way we draw lines around cities, poverty groups, and minorities.

We also have a carry-over of the industrial order. We have organized our educational systems the way factories were organized in the early twentieth century. Education has become almost immovable and un-reformable in some of our large systems. Finally, our conventional system of education is uncertain about what effective learning really is. How do you instruct and get children to learn? Sometimes you wonder whether it is going to be impossible within the present system when the children are sitting in factories, and when there is no inspiration, spiritual or otherwise, to move them.

Releasing Human Power

Now here is this panoply or canvas of changes that are going through the world. We have this explosive human energy coming into conflict with school systems that still carry on the traditions of the industrial period. How could you break into this? And I will ask the question directly, "What have you, Outward

Bound, got to offer? How can Outward Bound help in this change that we have to go through in an orderly and constructive way to release the human power that is available to us?"

I have watched Outward Bound as carefully as I possibly could and listened, and this is what I sense you have learned about learning and the capacity to help the educational system to change.

There is no learning without challenge and emotion. I think if you remember the things you learned the best, they were emotional in character. Mine was an embarrassment by a geography teacher who asked me to show which way the Niagara River flowed. Since I didn't know and the map was up in front of me, I said, "This way." And she said, "Young man, you can do what God can't, you can get the Niagara River to flow up the Falls!" That was an emotional experience for me—it was a hell of an embarrassment—but the emotion is part of it.

And so is the challenge. You learn because this obstacle is in front of you and it is real. Outward Bound has perfected in schools—city and otherwise—this business of getting people emotionally charged, getting them in a situation where their emotions are up and there is a challenge to meet.

Caring and Intimacy

A second quality of the Outward Bound experience is caring and intimacy. When I headed up a national commission on Hispanic education and talked to Hispanic parents, children, and teachers, I asked,

"What makes the difference? Why did you succeed, and why do your brothers sometimes fail?" The answer came back, "I met a caring person. Someone believed in me—a mother, a teacher, a taxi cab driver, neighbor. Somebody took an interest in and treated me as a worthy human being." Intimacy is an essential part of this. We cannot do it in the mass. Human beings only learn and are cared for in the small, and these are two qualities I find in your operations.

The third factor is a high prospect of success. This is critical. I was once asked what I would define as the essentials of a good education. I said, "First, my kid needs at least one person who cares. Second, that my kid gets a chance at success, to feel what it is like to be able to accomplish and to do something that they didn't expect they could." And when you watch the failure syndromes, they are the succession of experiences in which failure is the result, and it just deadens the capacity and willingness of the spirit and learning.

The fourth element is that learning happens in an environment where the collective and the individualistic come together. I'll never forget an exchange I had with one of the noted anthropologists of Mainland China, Fa Sha Tung. We became friends and finally, when he determined that I could take it, he said, "Paul, can we have an argument?" I said, "Go ahead."

Fa Sha Tung said, "You represent a civilization with at least two fatal tendencies and qualities for world society. First, your technological obsession."

The second thing he said that impressed me was, "You have the fatal flaw of individualism. We don't believe human potential is reached as an individual exercise and expression. We work as part of a community, and we will not say that potential is realized, unless the community realizes it along with the individual." We have perfected individualism, but we have not been able to do it yet as an expression also of community advancement. Outward Bound has done that.

The Value of Values

Finally, learning takes place—and you have taught us this—in an environment where values are clear and where the value of values is immediately demonstrable. Unless you hang on to that rope with the other guy, you're going to fall off the cliff. It is immediately apparent. Too often, we are sitting in a verbal environment in which we preach values— "Look out there, you children behave"—and there isn't any demonstrable evidence of the value of those values.

Caught in the Syndrome?

These are five generic qualities that Outward Bound represents, and while you do have something very important to contribute to the education and dialogue that is now going on, I have wondered, sometimes, whether you would get caught in the syndrome.

Somebody once said, "Educational experiments are doomed to success." There is wisdom to that. You perfect the experiment, you encapsulate it, you insulate it, you dogmatize it, and it becomes doctrinaire, and this is patent medicine. It never communicates, because people feel more excluded than helped by what something essentially constructive represents.

I wondered if Outward Bound would become another proprietary medicine, and would achieve its own doctrine, the bible according to whomever, and people would begin shying away from you, rather than seeing what you represent in those five qualities that I talked about. What I have seen as I've watched you and participated with you over time has encouraged me to think that was not going to happen. Somebody once said that the best test of efficiency is survival. Outward Bound has survived. More than that, it has grown. More than that, it has been continuously creative and experimental and reached out to new forms and expressions of communicating and transmitting these essential qualities that you have to contribute.

You have been very entrepreneurial. You also have a dedication to the principle of inclusion, instead of becoming as elitist as you could have become, and originally were. When I watch what you've been doing, orienting to the people who are not advantaged—the urban poor, the handicapped—I am really encouraged by the spirit of growth and creativity and dedication to all people, not just a few.

COLLABORATION

One last thing: I like your spirit of collaboration. I can imagine the temptation to patent your medicine, and to become very possessive of Outward Bound. "Damn those people who are imitating us, and are not giving us credit, who don't have all the standards that we have and who are committing all those lapses." You've been willing to tie in with other groups and share all those generic qualities that I talked about. You, as one organization, will never touch the whole world, but you can communicate the essence of who you are, and be generous and let other people carry on in the same tradition.

I cannot leave you without sermonizing a little bit. What can we use more of, from Outward Bound? One, a more articulate and—I don't like to use the word—aggressive participation in the educational dialogue. This last ten years in America, and for that matter around the world, have been full of the debate about where we ought to go in education. You have a tremendous amount to offer in that debate. You are not, as I hear it, audible. You are not articulate. And I am not talking about being evangelical about your organization. I am talking about what you essentially have to contribute to where education ought to be going.

The Missing Dimension

You are not audible, as I can hear it, in the debate over reform. Legislatures have been full of it in this country and elsewhere. Is there somebody from your organization or your spirit who is talking about these missing dimensions in contemporary education? I am not inviting you to get into the trivia of research; that is a full-employment business with low productivity. What I am encouraging you to be is a voice, where things are talked about and debated. That extra dimension badly needs talking and writing about in ways that are not possessive, but are sharing and giving.

We at the Graduate School of Education could use this voice, and I would like it from somebody who has a hands-on background and a capacity to articulate.

Let's work together.

EXPEDITIONARY LEARNING OUTWARD BOUND

Expeditionary Learning is a design for school reform that challenges kindergarten–twelfth-grade students to meet rigorous academic and character standards. Through professional development and technical assistance, we collaborate with the entire school staff to make schools safe, engaging communities where all students are expected to achieve more than they thought possible. A New American Schools design for comprehensive school improvement, Expeditionary Learning is built around ten design principles and five core practices that guide the teaching and learning in our schools.

EXPEDITIONARY LEARNING DESIGN PRINCIPLES[1]

Learning is an expedition into the unknown. Expeditions draw together personal experience and intellectual growth to promote self-discovery and the construction of knowledge. We believe that adults should guide students along this journey with care, compassion, and respect for their diverse learning styles, backgrounds, and needs. Addressing individual differences profoundly increases the potential for learning and creativity of each student.

Given fundamental levels of health, safety, and love, all people can and want to learn. We believe

Expeditionary Learning harnesses the natural passion to learn and is a powerful method for developing the curiosity, skills, knowledge, and courage needed to imagine a better world and work toward realizing it.

THE PRIMACY OF SELF-DISCOVERY

Learning happens best with emotion, challenge, and the requisite support. People discover their abilities, values, "grand passions," and responsibilities in situations that offer adventure and the unexpected. They must have tasks that require perseverance, fitness, craftsmanship, imagination, self-discipline, and significant achievement. A primary job of the educator is to help students overcome their fear and discover they have more in them than they think.

THE HAVING OF WONDERFUL IDEAS

Teach so as to build on children's curiosity about the world by creating learning situations that provide matter to think about, time to experiment, and time to make sense of what is observed. Foster a community where students' and adults' ideas are respected.

THE RESPONSIBILITY FOR LEARNING

Learning is both a personal, individually specific process of discovery and a social activity. Each of us learns within and for ourselves and as a part of a group. Every aspect of a school must encourage children, young people, and adults to become increasingly responsible for directing their own personal and collective learning.

Intimacy and Caring

Learning is fostered best in small groups where there is trust, sustained caring, and mutual respect among all members of the learning community. Keep schools and learning groups small. Be sure there is a caring adult looking after the progress of each child. Arrange for the older students to mentor the younger ones.

Success and Failure

All students must be assured a fair measure of success in learning in order to nurture the confidence and capacity to take risks and rise to increasingly difficult challenges. But it is also important to experience failure, to overcome negative inclinations, to prevail against adversity, and to learn to turn disabilities into opportunities.

Collaboration and Competition

Teach so as to join individual and group development so that the value of friendship, trust, and group endeavor is made manifest. Encourage students to compete, not against each other, but with their own personal best and with rigorous standards of excellence.

DIVERSITY AND INCLUSIVITY

Diversity and inclusivity in all groups dramatically increase richness of ideas, creative power, problem-solving ability, and acceptance of others. Encourage students to investigate, value, and draw upon their own different histories, talents, and resources together with those of other communities and cultures. Keep the schools and learning groups heterogeneous.

THE NATURAL WORLD

A direct and respectful relationship with the natural world refreshes the human spirit and reveals the important lessons of recurring cycles and cause and effect. Students learn to become stewards of the earth and of the generations to come.

SOLITUDE AND REFLECTION

Solitude, reflection, and silence replenish our energies and open our minds. Be sure students have time alone to explore their own thoughts, make their own connections, and create their own ideas. Then give them opportunity to exchange their reflections with each other and with adults.

Service and Compassion

We are crew, not passengers, and are strengthened by acts of consequential service to others. One of a school's primary functions is to prepare its students with the attitudes and skills to learn from and be of service to others.

---

[1] The above principles have been informed by Kurt Hahn's "Seven Laws of Salem," by Paul Ylvisaker's "The Missing Dimension," and by Eleanor Duckworth's *"The Having of Wonderful Ideas" and Other Essays on Teaching and Learning* (New York: Teachers College Press, 1987).

Expeditionary Learning
Outward Bound
100 Mystery Point Road
Garrison, NY 10524
(914) 424-4000
www.elob.org

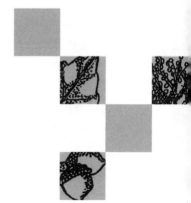